D1571150

Sermon Warm-ups

21 Lead-in Skits

Lori Lee Triplett

CSS Publishing Company, Inc., Lima, Ohio

SERMON WARM-UPS

Copyright © 2002 by
CSS Publishing Company, Inc.
Lima, Ohio

The original purchaser may photocopy material in this publication for use as it was in-
tended (i.e., worship material for worship use; educational material for classroom use;
dramatic material for staging or production). No additional permission is required from
the publisher for such copying by the original purchaser only. Inquiries should be ad-
dressed to: Permissions, CSS Publishing Company, Inc., P.O. Box 4503, Lima, Ohio 45802-
4503.

For more information about CSS Publishing Company resources, visit our website at
www.csspub.com or e-mail us at custserv@csspub.com or call (800) 241-4056.

ISBN 0-7880-1951-1   PRINTED IN U.S.A.

I dedicate this to God.
May He use my life
and talents for His will.

Table Of Contents

Waiting

Scriptures: Acts 2:1-21 or John 16:4b-15
Romans 8:12-17 or John 3:1-17

Cast Of Characters
Church Secretary: either sex and any age older than college
Church Member: either sex and any age
Music Director: either sex and any age older than college
Mystery Man/Jenkins: an average-looking man

(The lights come up on a secretary busy at the church office desk. The member rushes in)

Member: *(Excitedly)* Listen, we need to call the police! There is a guy sitting out in a car, in the church parking lot.

Secretary: The police?

Member: Yes, right now. Quick, call 911.

Secretary: But what am I reporting to the police? *(Picks up the phone and dials)*

Member: That we have a weird man in the parking lot, and they should come move him along. Arrest him for trespassing, whatever, just get him out of the parking lot.

Secretary: *(Hangs up the phone in disgust)* How do you know he is a weird man?

Member: Because I sat in my car and watched him, sitting in his car.

Secretary: So, you were both sitting in your cars in the church parking lot. That makes him a weirdo?

Member: Yes, because he's not a member here. I have been a member here for many years, and I know he is not a member. Therefore he should not be sitting in the church parking lot. He might be trying to "case the joint" and steal from us.

Secretary: But why would you think he was going to steal from us, if he's just sitting in the parking lot? *(Sarcastically)* Did he have shifty eyes?

Member: You know, I couldn't really see his eyes; they were shut most of the time.

Director: *(Enters, carrying music and a baton)* Say, did anyone else notice the guy sitting in the parking lot?

Secretary: Oh, yes, I am currently receiving a full report.

Member: Yes, I asked her to call 911, but she just hung up. Perhaps you can convince her of the need to take action.

Director: Well, I don't know if we need to call the police. I think maybe we should call an ambulance, or doctor. He looked like he was sick or something. I mean, he was just sitting there with his eyes closed —

Member: See, I told you —

Director: And his lips are moving. How long has he been sitting there?

Member: For most of the morning. I watched him from the safety of my car. I think he is planning on robbing us.

Director: Well, there has been a rash of church robberies lately.

Member: Did you see any weapons? I think the police should know what they are up against. Perhaps they will need to bring a SWAT team. That is *if* we call 911. Perhaps as Director of Music here, you can overrule —

Secretary: Wait a minute; calm down. Did anyone try to talk to the man? Maybe he just needs someone to talk with —

Member: Then he should seek professional help, see a psychologist if necessary, not just sit in our parking lot.

Mystery Man: *(A very ordinary man dressed in a suit enters, unnoticed by the other three)* Excuse me —

(Member screams, grabs Secretary's arm, and jumps down behind Secretary for protection. Director drops his music to the floor, backs up, and wields his baton like a sword, attempting to protect himself)

Member: It's him! Call 911! Call 911!

Secretary: I can't; you're holding my arm. *(Member lets go immediately, and curls up on the floor. Secretary immediately holds her hand out to shake hands)* Hello, Mr. Jenkins, isn't it? It's nice to see you again.

Member: *(Gets up from the floor)* You know this man?

Mystery Man: I'm sorry; is something wrong here? Perhaps I could be of assistance? *(Jenkins leans down to begin picking up the scattered music)*

Director: *(Puts the baton down, trying to act nonchalant)* No, no, nothing wrong. Here, let me do that. *(Takes the music Jenkins has already picked up)*

Mystery Man: I wonder if I might speak with the minister again. I know I'm not a member here, so —

Member: Ah, I was right.

Secretary: Our minister would be happy to speak with you again. It doesn't matter if you're a member or not. Unfortunately, he's not here right now. He's visiting someone in the hospital.

Mystery Man: Oh, well, I was afraid he wasn't here. I was waiting in the parking lot for him to pull up. He helped me a great deal the other day. Well, I'll just go back to my car and wait a little longer.

Member: You've been here before?

Mystery Man: Yes, about a week ago. *(Pauses)* I was just recently downsized. I was at a loss —

Member: You were fired?

Mystery Man: *(Reluctantly)* Yes, actually it was several months ago. I was unsure of what to do.

Director: Sounds like a difficult time.

Mystery Man: Very. Last week I prayed for the first time since I was a child. I was driving by the church after yet another unsuccessful job interview ... something just made me pull into the parking lot, and pray.

Member: Well, I'm so glad. *(Sits down)* Our parking lot is open to everyone, of course — no gated security for us.

Mystery Man: Your minister saw me praying in the parking lot, and invited me inside, so that we could pray together.

Director: Hey! That's a great idea!

Mystery Man: Yes, well, I'm new at this waiting game, so it was nice to have someone to wait with me. The minister is helping me while I wait for guidance. Well, I'll just —

Secretary: Mr. Jenkins, please have a seat. You can wait here.

Director: Sure, we'll wait with you.

Mystery Man: Thanks, but it might take a while. I'm afraid I'm waiting for more than just your minister. *(Sits, then addresses the member)* Say, I noticed you sitting in the parking lot too. Were you waiting for the minister, also?

Member: *(Sheepishly)* Not exactly.

Mystery Man: Oh, I see. So, what are you waiting for?

(Blackout)

The Adoption Agency

Scriptures: Romans 8:12-17
John 3:1-17

Cast Of Characters
Agency Director: male or female older than college age
Leslie Tunston: female in her thirties or older, married to Jason
Jason Tunston: male in his thirties or older, married to Leslie

---

(As the lights come up the Agency Director is escorting the couple into his/her office)

Director: Mr. and Mrs. Tunston, please come into my office.

Jason: Feel free to call us Jason and Leslie.

Director: Thank you, I will. Please have a seat. *(Gestures for the couple to have a seat, and they do)* As you are aware, I'm the director for the Adoption Agency, and it's my job to conduct the final interview. We just want to make sure that everything is in order and all of the policies have been followed.

Leslie: Oh, of course, we can understand. I can't tell you how thrilled we are to come this close to reaching our goal of adopting.

Director: I'll just make a quick final look-through on the questionnaires. *(Flips through the forms in a folder)*

Jason: Is everything satisfactory on the forms?

13

Leslie: If we need to provide more info, we'd be happy to do so. Please don't deny us the opportunity to adopt! If we missed a question or didn't answer it to your —

Director: Please, Jason and Leslie, I'm sure you have nothing to worry about.

Jason: I'm sorry if we seem a little anxious.

Leslie: We just don't want anything to go wrong, now that we've come this far.

Director: Well, you seem to have all your paperwork well in hand. *(Both prospective parents give a sigh of relief)* I just want to ask a couple more questions. *(Both parents tense up again)* You are aware that most of our adoptees are quite a bit older than average. Generally the younger ones have already been selected.

Jason: Yes, we understand that. It's not a problem.

Leslie: We specifically wanted to adopt someone older.

Director: I see from the answers you gave that you are actively involved in the church?

Leslie: Oh, yes! I can't imagine life without our church family.

Jason: We definitely try to put God first in our lives.

Director: Yes, well that sounds wonderful. I must tell you that this is my favorite part of my job, after all the forms have been completed and we have the final interview. *(Gives them a big grin)* So, would you like to look through some pictures and get their profiles?

Jason: You mean?

Director: Yes, I think you'll be wonderful —

Leslie: It's really happening! Thank you, God!

Director: We have three available for adoption. There is Jonathan, Teresa, and Thelma. *(Shifts through photos and brief bios)*

Jason: What are their interests?

Leslie: We thought it might be helpful if we had something in common.

Jason: You know, to give us an idea of what we could do together.

Director: Of course, that's a wonderful idea and a very successful way of finding a "good match." Jonathan likes to watch football, enjoys photography, and loves the outdoors.

Jason: Oh, he sounds great!

Leslie: Oh, I don't know. I don't like to do any of those things.

Director: Well, Teresa loves to shop, enjoys going to movies, and has a weakness for chocolate.

Leslie: She sounds perfect!

Jason: I don't think so.

Director: Thelma loves to read all kinds of books and visit the library —

Leslie: I don't read all that much.

Jason: We don't even have a library card.

Director: Well, then, perhaps Thelma would be better suited with someone else.

Jason: *(Says simultaneously with Leslie)* I think we should pick Jonathan. Leslie, I —

Leslie: *(Says simultaneously with Jason)* I think we should pick Teresa. Jason, how —

Director: *(Sees a fight brewing)* Well, perhaps we should —

Jason: I think we should go with Jonathan.

Leslie: And I still think we could help Teresa more.

Director: Perhaps there is another answer, if you're willing?

Jason: What?

Director: Why don't you work with both? Jason, you would relate more to Jonathan and be his mentor.

Leslie: And I could help Teresa. That's a wonderful idea!

Jason: If you think we can handle the responsibility, I'm willing.

Director: Oh, I'm sure you'll both do a great job. We've found this program very successful at helping new Christians grow. Let me check their ages to see if that makes a difference. Jonathan was born in 1960, so he's a little over forty but he accepted Christ just last month. And Teresa was born in 1973, but she gave herself to Jesus ... last week. These two God's children are very new and I'm sure either one of them would benefit from your spiritual knowledge and guidance. The mentors seem to benefit as well, as is so often the case when we help others.

Jason: When can we start?

Leslie: Yes, I can't wait to meet them both.

Director: Let me give you their telephone numbers and you can give them a call.

(Blackout)

Sundays

Scriptures: 2 Corinthians 4:5-12
Mark 2:23—3:6

Cast Of Characters
Jane: friend of Sara's and a similar age
Sara: friend of Jane's and a similar age

(It is Sunday morning and people are gathered drinking coffee/tea and having fellowship)

Jane: I love this church fellowship time!

Sara: Me too! I get to catch up with my friends, and have some coffee to wake up.

Jane: So, how was work this week?

Sara: It was boring as usual. How about your week?

Jane: Oh, it was great! No one's lunch got stolen this week.

Sara: Someone steals your lunches?

Jane: Yes, for about three months now. Some people have stopped bringing their lunch. What's the point if you're not going to get to eat it? Sally, one of the secretaries, tried to set a trap for the thief by putting red pepper on the outside of everyone's lunch.

Sara: Did it work?

Jane: Not exactly, because all of us ended up sneezing. It was worth a try. At this point we've tried just about everything.

Sara: I wonder why it stopped this week? Was the thief on vacation?

Jane: A good thought, but no one was on vacation. I decided to try a little honey to catch the fly, if you know what I mean.

Sara: You put honey all over everyone's food?

Jane: No, silly, I took an extra lunch for that person to eat.

Sara: How did the thief know that was his or her lunch?

Jane: I labeled it.

Sara: You wrote thief on the bag?

Jane: No, it didn't seem politically correct.

Sara: Someone's stealing your lunches for three months and you're worrying about what's PC?

Jane: Well, what if someone is starving? I mean, maybe they can't afford to buy a lunch.

Sara: Well, they must have some money because they work there.

Jane: But what if they have a lot of medical expenses? Or maybe they've hit on really hard times, like trying to pay off their school loans or something.

Sara: So, how long did it take you to come up with that explanation?

Jane: Anyway, an extra lunch a day won't kill my budget and we had such peace at the office this week. No one was running around cussing or agitated or threatening to kill the lunch stealer. It was worth it.

Sara: So, how long are you going to keep this up? And, I repeat: How did the thief know which lunch to take?

Jane: I labeled it "extra lunch." And I guess I'll keep doing it until the day that the lunch is not eaten. *(Sara is stunned into silence)* No comment?

Sara: I'm stunned. Give me a minute to recover. So, how come you weren't after revenge like everyone else? What happened to an eye-for-an-eye and all that stuff?

Jane: I read the New Testament. Sometimes it puts a new interpretation on things.

Sara: Say, I'm glad you brought that up. Jane, this is really important. I need to ask you a tough question.

Jane: Oh, no! Knowing you and with a set-up like that, I'm in real trouble. Is this a philosophical, hypothetical, or biblical context question?

Sara: What are you doing the rest of today after church?

Jane: That's the tough question?

Sara: Just part one. It's a multiple part question.

Jane: I'll probably read my Bible a little and then write a letter to God about my week. I'm going to relax most of the day. If God with all of his powers rested on the seventh day, then I figure I need rest too. Then maybe I'll go to a movie. How about you?

Sara: I was going to the grocery store, the drug store, and the discount outlet. There are these really cute shoes I want. But I figure that's okay, right? I'm buying food. I can't starve, right? And then I need to pick up my prescriptions. I can't do without those.

Jane: So, what category does buying cute shoes fall under?

Sara: The same category as you going to a movie?

Jane: I was afraid you would point that out.

Sara: I'm having a little trouble rationalizing the shoe part of my errands. But I figure I'm already out and ...

Jane: So, did you want my help rationalizing the errand away or is there another part to this question?

Sara: There's another part. I know how you're supposed to keep a day holy. But I thought maybe in this modern-day world we didn't really have to honor it or it doesn't apply to everyone.

Jane: I think it applies to everyone, even animals.

Sara: Or maybe there was something in the New Testament that said, don't worry about it. I mean, some people have to work in a hospital, or what about a minister.

Jane: But those people are doing good, performing a service. There is something in the New Testament that addresses that issue ... but I hope they just pick a different day to rest and keep as holy. Sara, why are you asking these questions?

Sara: Because ... I decided I was going to read my Bible a little each day this year.

Jane: That's a great idea!

Sara: But sometimes I have a hard time applying what I read to my everyday life. I mean, some of it just isn't practical.

Jane: Yes, I know what you mean. But do you really think it isn't practical, or that we choose to find a way not to follow it?

(Blackout)

Questions

Scriptures: 2 Corinthians 4:13—5:1
2 Corinthians 5:6-10

(This can be done as a readers' theatre or memorized with three or six people. If three are used, simply double A/D, B/E, C/F)

A: Okay, I thought I was doing the right thing. I reported the other cashier for stealing. But now I'm the one without the job, because she blamed me. How am I supposed to pay my bills? I wish I'd never said anything.

B: So, I have this wonderful opportunity with a brand new company. But is it really what I want to do? I really like living here.

C: I don't have a clue about life. I just show up. What am I supposed to do?

All: Is God really there?

D: This praying stuff doesn't always work. I just don't get it.

E: So, I can't decide if I really like this person or not.

F: I like my life just the way it is. I like my job. I have nothing to complain about. Don't change anything, okay? *(Pauses)* So, why is something missing?

All: Does God listen?

A: Okay, I'm waiting for you to open some new doors. Can you please show me the way to go?

B: But if I move, I'll lose all my friends. I won't be able to call in my favors. But it's the chance of a lifetime. Of course, I don't really know much about this new company.

C: Life is tough enough, and then something really bad happens.

All: Does God care?

D: Step one, give thanks. Thanks! Is that all it takes to pray? *(Consults a book)* No, it's a three-step process.

E: Love should be special, different.

F: I should probably take more risks, but how do I know when is the right time?

All: Does God really hear me?

A: Okay, so what should I do at this point, today, now? Do I call on the unemployment office? An agency?

B: I can make a list of pros and cons. Maybe that will help me decide whether to move or not.

C: So, I'm waiting for the next bad thing to happen. It's been a couple of days. Oh, no, does that mean any second now?

All: Does God send signs anymore?

D: The list is as follows: give thanks, ask for forgiveness, ask for what you want. I should be really good with the last part.

E: Love should be perfect. Is that possible?

F: Well, I'm getting off my schedule. That's what leads to discontent. Stick to a schedule and you'll be amazed at what can be done.

All: I wish someone was here right now.

A: Will an employment agency even talk to me after they hear what I'm accused of?

B: But which pros and cons? Work or personal?

C: Don't ever ask what is the worst thing that can happen. Trust me, I've been there.

All: I need some help here.

D: Please forgive me, I'm sure I've done something wrong today. Well, if not today, then at least yesterday. Great, now I get to ask for what I want!

E: Unconditional love is about as perfect as you can get. But where in the world can you find that?

All: Can't someone show me the way?

(Blackout)

Raging

Scriptures: 2 Corinthians 6:1-13
Mark 4:35-41

(This stand-alone monologue should be done as simply as possible, one on one with God)

Oh, God! I don't get it. I don't get how you could take my husband away from me. He died in an accident on the way to work. It is not like he was committing some terrible sin and you needed to stop him from doing the act. We stood in front of you and made a vow to grow old together. Neither one of us went back on our word.

And what about my children? What am I supposed to tell them? They're both still in grade school. How am I going to explain it to them, when I can't even explain it to myself? *(Tries several different stories to imaginary children)* Sorry, but God needs Daddy in heaven. Or Daddy's purpose on earth is served, so he went to heaven. Your daddy had completed his spiritual journey here on earth, and so now he's with Jesus. God needs people of all ages and all types in heaven. *(Back to God)* What if they think they did something so wrong, and that's why you took their daddy? Did they have to learn this lesson so early in life? By the way, what lessons are we supposed to be learning right now?

Can't you see? I'm not ready to let go of my husband. I don't see why I should. All my other friends still have their husbands, but not me. How am I going to raise two children by myself? How am I going to provide for them and take care of them too? It wasn't supposed to be like this! What did I do, so bad, that you would punish me like this? Why, God? Why?

I know I'm not supposed to wonder why. What wisdom do you see that I don't comprehend? What purpose in your great world does the death of my husband serve? If you can't bring my children's father back, can you at least help us to understand? Can you give me peace? The peace like the disciples felt when they saw Jesus calm the storm. They didn't understand it either, but they understood that you controlled it all. Can you calm the storm in me?

(Blackout)

Attitude

Scriptures: 2 Corinthians 8:7-15
Genesis 4:3-10 (alternative)

Cast Of Characters
Narrator: male or female, any age
Cain: the older brother
Abel: the younger brother

(Narrator, seated to one side, opens an oversized storybook and reads. The brothers act out the story and start with their backs to the audience)

Narrator: Once upon a time, in a land far, far away, there lived two brothers. Cain was the firstborn. *(Cain turns around and swaggers forward with attitude of a major ego)* Now, as the firstborn he was doted on by his parents. Adam and Eve had given much thanks to God for the gift of a child. Next Abel was born. *(Abel turns around and steps forward unpretentiously)* Of course, Adam and Eve loved both of the children and raised them according to God's word. Cain grew up and decided to work the soil. *(He steps to the center area)* His day consisted of morning prayers.

Cain: *(Lazily as if he doesn't really mean it)* Dear God, thanks for this day. Help me to grow some great crops. Yada, yada! Amen. *(Pauses)* Whatever!

Narrator: *(Sarcastically)* The depth of his feeling was quite overwhelming.

31

Cain: Hey! I thought you were supposed to be reading a story, not making editorial comments.

Narrator: Well, excuse me! *(Returns to the story)* Day after day, Cain worked his fields and raised his crops.

Cain: *(Starts miming hoeing)* See, I'm not such a bad guy. I do my work day after day.

Narrator: Abel grew up and decided to keep flocks. He too started his day with prayers.

Abel: *(Steps forward and kneels to pray)* Dear God, thank you for all the many gifts you have given me. Please help me to do my work today in a way which brings you glory. And if it is your will, please help my animals to grow and multiply. Please be with Cain and help him to work the soil for your glory. Amen. *(Pauses)* I hope my prayer pleases you.

Cain: Hey, cool! My crops should really grow since two of us are praying for them.

Narrator: Day after day, Abel worked his flocks and watched them grow and multiply, *(Abel mimes feeding sheep or shearing)* stopping to give thanks throughout the day. Then it was time to bring their offerings to the Lord. Abel carefully selected the best of his work and presented it to the Lord.

Abel: *(Chooses, and then offers both hands toward the sky)* Dear God, here is my firstborn and best of my flock. May it please you!

Narrator: And God was pleased, and looked on Abel with favor. Cain can be seen selecting too. He is selecting grain or vegetables with mold on them.

Cain: Part of it's still good; you just need to cut around it. I mean, it's not like you're really going to eat it. So, why waste the good stuff?

Narrator: The Lord compared the two offerings and found Cain's lacking. So, God did not look on Cain with favor. Cain was very angry!

Cain: What's your problem? I gave you some stuff.

Narrator: But God realized that Cain had *an attitude*. Even though Cain had prayed and given to the Lord, he had not done it in the right way. If Cain had done it in the right way, God would have accepted it. God told Cain that he needed to be very careful or sin would take over his life.

Cain: Oh, give me a break! I've had it with this. Every day I prayed and when the time was right I gave my offering. It's not fair that God likes my brother better.

Narrator: So, Cain went to visit Abel and suggested that maybe he would like to visit Cain's land. *(Cain crosses to Abel and talks with him, pats him on the back)*

Abel: Oh, sure I'd love to come for a visit. Thanks for inviting me. *(They walk together to Cain's land)*

Narrator: So Cain and Abel walked together in the fields. Then suddenly Cain attacked his brother and killed him. *(Cain jumps on Abel and knocks him to the ground. Cain then drags Abel offstage, before returning)* Cain immediately went back to working his fields. The next morning, Cain started his usual morning prayers.

Cain: Dear God, thanks for this day. Help me to grow some great crops. Yada —

Narrator: But God interrupted the prayer and asked, "Where is Abel?"

Cain: Like, I'm not in charge of him, man! Today's not my day.

Narrator: God was very upset and could hear Abel's blood screaming out to him. So, God put a mark on Cain, forced him to leave his fields, and wander. But do you think Cain felt sorry for what he had done?

Cain: I can't bear this! *(Trudges off)*

Narrator: And our story ends with Cain still thinking of only himself. The moral of this story is: *attitude is the real you! (Closes the storybook)* So, how's your attitude today?

(Blackout)

A Thorn

Scriptures: 2 Corinthians 12:2-10
Mark 6:1-6

Cast Of Characters
Jessica: a sick singer who wants to make a career singing
Rachel: a minister and Jessica's best friend

(Jessica and Rachel are in the living room sipping on canned sodas)

Rachel: So, how are you doing today?

Jessica: *(Crabby)* Well, at least you didn't ask, how are *we* doing today. How should I be doing? I'm a singer that can't sing.

Rachel: Bad day, huh? What does the doctor say?

Jessica: That I should be thankful my speaking voice was unaffected by the damage.

Rachel: Throat cancer can be a very devastating disease. Does he think he got all of it?

Jessica: Yes, for now anyway. I'll have to watch it and go back for check-ups.

Rachel: Maybe you just need to give it some more time to heal.

Jessica: It's healed all that it's going to heal. The voice I have now is what I'm stuck with. How am I supposed to make my living? I mean, my career was just starting to take off. Do you know I signed autographs after my last performance? And now, this! I can't even hit the high notes.

Rachel: So sing low notes. Use the lower register of your voice.

Jessica: Rachel, it's not that simple. My agent has marketed me based on certain skills, like thrilling high notes and vocal dexterity. I don't have those anymore. In fact, my agent called me yesterday. I guess he's not my agent anymore.

Rachel: Oh, Jessica, I'm sorry. That's why you're so upset today, isn't it?

Rachel: Yeah, I guess I'm going job hunting. Starting a new career. So, how's your career going?

Rachel: Wonderful! I love being a minister, and my congregation is so thoughtful. They really made me feel at home.

Jessica: I always figured you'd go back to your home church.

Rachel: I thought about it. I even went back and interviewed for a position there.

Jessica: And?

Rachel: Everyone still called me Rach, and teased me about every little sin I ever committed as a child.

Jessica: Funny! That's not how I remember things. In fact, I was the troublemaker, not you.

Rachel: Well, it became clear to me they were not going to listen to what I preached, if all they were thinking about was some silly incident from my childhood.

36

Jessica: No respect, huh?

Rachel: I decided if they couldn't honor what I had made of my life, what I had become, I would go elsewhere.

Jessica: Well, at least you know what you're going to do with your life. I don't have a clue.

Rachel: Have you thought about asking God what he wants you to do?

Jessica: Me, ask God? Rachel, I didn't even go to church services except on holidays.

Rachel: You were in the youth group.

Jessica: Yeah, so I could sing and stuff — that was it. You don't think I listened to the lesson, do you? I was daydreaming about being a star.

Rachel: You were great at singing those praise songs. Do you sing those anymore?

Jessica: No, I haven't sung a religious song since high school.

Rachel: So, why don't you try one of those now? I know they aren't as difficult as what you're used to singing, but I bet you could still sing those.

Jessica: Rachel, I love to sing. I love to hear my voice soar. And now, God has taken that away from me. So, singing songs of praise to him doesn't strike me as a good idea right now.

Rachel: So, sing songs of anguish to him if you want. Just so you communicate with him, talk to him. This is the perfect time to start your relationship with God. Ask him what he wants you to do in life, since he's taken your career away.

Jessica: We'll see.

Rachel: I brought a CD of praise songs for you.

Jessica: What did you do that for?

Rachel: It seemed like a good idea this morning when I was praying to God about you. *(Sets the CD on the table)*

Jessica: I won't listen to it, so you might as well take it back.

Rachel: Well, I've got to be going. If you want to talk to me about
anything again, just give me a call. *(Leaves without the CD)*

Jessica: Yeah, well, thanks for coming. Bye! *(Watches Rachel leave
and stares at the recording)* Oh, Rachel, you never could just leave
me to mope in my misery. *(Picks up the disc or tape and pops it
into a player. One possible song is "This Thorn" by Twyla Paris,
or another song of the director's choosing)*

(Blackout)

The Inheritance

Scriptures: Ephesians 1:3-14
                   Mark 6:14-29

Cast Of Characters
Attorney: middle-aged, can be male or female
Jojo: the youngest and brashest of the sisters
Wanda: the middle sister, and the most calm
Nancy: the oldest of the sisters, used to taking charge

(The lights come up on an attorney reading the will to three women seated in a row)

Attorney: In witness whereof, I have subscribed my name to my Last Will and Testament, consisting of five typewritten pages —

Jojo: I don't think you need to finish it. We got the gist.

Attorney: It was, of course, duly witnessed and signed. Please feel free to examine the original and I will have a copy made for each of you to peruse.

Wanda: There must be some sort of mistake.

Attorney: I'm sorry, but —

Nancy: There's no mistake. It seems perfectly clear to me. Father left everything to Wanda. Why he thought she should handle things instead of me ...

Jojo: Well, I don't think she should start counting the money quite yet. *(To Wanda)* Don't even think you're going to get it all. I'll contest it.

Nancy: If you want to waste your money trying to break the will go ahead, but I think it's pointless.

Wanda: *(To the attorney)* Did he explain to you why?

Attorney: Yes, somewhat. You see —

Jojo: This I gotta hear. There is no reason that she should get all the money. I deserve at least a third, if not half.

Nancy: What is wrong with your math? Why should you get half?

Jojo: Because you never did anything for him. So, Wanda and I should split the money. You should get nothing.

Wanda: Excuse me, can you help us to understand? Did he give you any reasons?

Attorney: He did leave a letter of explanation.

Jojo: Like there is anything that could explain this situation.

Nancy: Dad didn't owe you anything. He gave you the down payment on your house. That was your share.

Jojo: That was years ago and it doesn't equal what you got. You got a college educ —

Attorney: Ladies, please! I know you are upset —

Nancy: Of course, I'm upset. It's only Wanda that's perfectly fine.

Jojo: That's because she got all the money.

Wanda: Please, both of you, stop this! Our father's wishes deserve to be respected. He was a good man and tried to help many people. It's not like I get the money personally.

Jojo: He was never home for us. He was always traveling with that evangelistic tour.

Nancy: He was trying to spread the word —

Jojo: By neglecting us?

Wanda: Could you please read the letter of explanation?

Attorney: *(Takes the letter out of his briefcase and begins to read)* Dear daughters. Herein lie the —

Jojo: I don't need to hear any more legal mumbo-jumbo. Can't you just tell us in plain English the scoop?

Attorney: Very well. He wanted his estate used to continue his work. As a reminder, Wanda doesn't really get the money. She is just in charge of dispensing it. Your father felt that all of you had been left a greater inheritance than he could ever give you.

Jojo: What on earth are you talking about? You just told me I got nothing!

(Blackout)

The Food

Scriptures: Mark 6:30-34, 53-56
John 6:1-21

Cast Of Characters
Kristen: female, college age or older
Linda: female, older than Kristen

(The lights come up on a one-room efficiency apartment. The furniture is old and beat-up. Kristen is frantically digging through everything to come up with some money for food. She tosses a few pennies on the table)

Kristen: Oh, yeah! Here's some change. *(Digs through the bottom of a huge bag)* A dime and a nickel. Well, I'll add it to the pile. *(Tosses the coins onto the table and sits down. She begins to pray)* Dear God: Thank you for helping me get over my illness. I am working very hard to pay off all my medical bills. God, I really need your help. I don't think eighteen cents is going to last me through the week, because I need groceries. I've tried really hard to cut out all the luxuries. I've moved into this studio apartment. I stick to just the basics of food. I try to live my life by following Jesus' teachings, but I know I make mistakes ... I just ... I just wanted to have some breakfast this morning before I went to work, okay? But I can see that my eighteen cents is not going to cut it. I guess I'll just go without. It won't be the first time. But, this is the second morning in a row, and I'm getting really hungry. Please, God, help me to find some money. Thank you for listening to me. Amen. *(Gets up again and really begins to hunt, throwing the pillows off*

43

the sleeper sofa, looking through trinket boxes, and whatever props are available) Where else can I look? *(Dejected, she sits on the floor)* Well, I guess the answer to my prayer is ... no. *(Glances at her watch)* Well, I still have some time before work. It sure takes less time to get ready in the mornings, if you don't eat breakfast. Maybe I'll make a grocery list. *(Sarcastically)* Just in case a check comes in the mail, or I win the lottery. *(Gets a pad and pencil, writing as she goes)* I need bread, milk ... no, I can do without milk. *(Crosses that off the list)* Peanut butter ... it does cost a couple of dollars a jar, but I can stretch it for about a week's meals. Potatoes ... I'll do without the sour cream or butter. It really isn't too bad with just salt and pepper. *(Pauses)* Maybe I should go see one of those agencies again. They helped me last month. Oh, no, I can't. They only help you so many times. Okay, what else do I absolutely have to have? Macaroni and cheese. Oh, no, I can't get that, I'd have to have milk and butter. Oh, just forget it. *(Throws the pencil down)* God, please, if it's not your will for me to have some money right now, could I at least have some food? *(Pauses)* Maybe he doesn't send food anymore. *(The phone rings, and she picks it up)* Hello? ... Hi, Linda ... No, you didn't wake me. I was just getting ready for work. Aren't you usually driving the commute by now? ... Oh, well, yes, I suppose those cell phones do come in handy ... You want to stop by now! On your way to work? Well, okay, I mean, I have a few minutes. Is everything okay? ... Well, couldn't you give me a hint what this is about before you get here? ... Okay, whatever, I'll see you in a few minutes. Bye. *(Hangs up the phone and glances around the room. She frantically begins to straighten the room up)* Oh, no, I made such a mess this morning. I wonder what she is stopping by for. She could have told me something. Maybe it's about the program we're doing together for church. *(The doorbell rings, and Kristen quickly goes to answer)* Hey, Linda, what's going on? I thought you didn't like to get up mornings.

Linda: Hello, Kristen! Here, this is for you. *(Carries a big cardboard box and plops it on the table, talking non-stop)* Well, I took your advice about getting up early, to get a few things done. And you're right; it makes a big difference. Of course, I end up going to bed earlier too, but that's okay.

Kristen: Well, I'm glad you like it.

Linda: I even went to the grocery store before work today. Isn't that shocking?

Kristen: Yes, are you sure you're feeling all right?

Linda: Great, I feel great. I have a lot more energy and —

Kristen: I'm not sure you needed any more energy.

Linda: Oh, you can never have too much energy. Anyway, the reason I'm here is that the grocery store this morning had all these buy one get one free specials. And since I live alone, two of every item is not going to do me a lot of good. It will just spoil.

Kristen: *(Not wanting to accept charity)* Oh, no —

Linda: So anyway, I put a bunch of stuff in the box. If you don't need it, then pass it on to someone who does. *(Heads for the door)*

Kristen: Linda, wait a minute. You can't —

Linda: Oh, yes, I can. And I don't want to hear any nonsense about you paying me for half. Now I've got to go, or I'll be late for work.

Kristen: Well, I will pay you. Next time I see you.

Linda: Don't be silly. Just promise me you won't let the food go to waste. I'll see you next week at the program meeting.

Kristen: Are we still meeting at the church at 7:00?

Linda: Yes, and don't forget to bring your ideas. *(Leaves)*

Kristen: Linda, thank you.

Linda: *(Offstage)* For what? You don't even know if you'll like what's in the box. Got to go, bye!

Kristen: *(Yells so that Linda who's leaving can hear)* I'm sure I'll like it, whatever it is. See you, bye. *(Crosses back to the box, opens it, and begins pulling out items)* Oh, my gosh, look at this. I can't believe this! There's bread, milk, macaroni and cheese, butter, and peanut butter. She even brought potatoes, and sour cream. Oh, what a treat, sour cream. Everything I needed plus a treat. But, how did she know? *(Pauses)* I guess you do still provide food. Thank you, God.

(Blackout)

The Committee

Scripture: Ephesians 4:1-16

Cast Of Characters
Janet Jason: female, older than college age
Mr. Snictnity: older, detail-oriented male
Minister: male or female, middle-aged
Mr./Ms. Jones: male or female, middle-aged architect
Mrs. Van Zahnt: older, wealthy church member

(The lights come up on a round table, with a semi-circle of chairs facing the audience. A refreshment table is off to one side. Mr. Snictnity is already seated, with his coffee. Janet Jason enters immediately)

Janet: Hello. Oh, I don't believe I've actually met you before, although, I've seen you around the church. I'm Janet Jason. *(Holds out her arm to shake hands)*

Snictnity: *(Rises)* Hello, I am Mr. Snictnity. *(Takes her hand to shake, then pulls a hankie out of his pocket, and proceeds to wipe off his hands)* That's with two *n*'s, two *i*'s, and two *t*'s.

Janet: Uh, thanks, I'll remember that. *(Crosses over to the side refreshment table, getting a glass of water and a cookie)* Can I get you a refill on your coffee, while I get my water?

Snictnity: No, thank you. I limit the amount of coffee I can have per evening.

Janet: Oh, okay. *(Joins him at the table and sits)* I'm kind of excited about this committee meeting, since it's my first one here. Have you met the architect yet?

Snictnity: No, and unless the architect arrives within the next minute he/she will be late. This meeting is scheduled to start at 7 p.m.

Janet: Well, yes, but perhaps —

Minister: *(Enters with the architect carrying blueprints)* Good evening. Hi, Janet, good to see you here. Let me introduce you to Mr./Ms. Jones. *(Jones and Janet shake hands)* Hello, Mr. Snictnity, glad you could make the meeting. This is Mr./Ms. Jones. *(The minister knows better than to shake hands with Snictnity. However, Jones shakes hands with Snictnity, who promptly wipes his hands off on his hankie again)*

Snictnity: That's with two *n*'s, two *i*'s, and two *t*'s.

Jones: Uh, how interesting.

Snictnity: Shall we go ahead and get started? I have 7 p.m. and counting.

Minister: Well, is Mrs. Van Zahnt here yet?

Janet: No, I don't believe so. At least I haven't seen her.

Minister: Maybe we'll just wait a few minutes. Mr./Ms. Jones, can I get you a cup of coffee or ice water to drink? We also have some cookies.

Jones: A cup of coffee would be great.

Minister: *(Pours coffee for both)* Mr. Snictnity, have you had your evening's limit yet?

Snictnity: Oh, yes, so good of you to remember, I —

Mrs. Van Zahnt: Hello, everyone. *(Stops, and hits a pose to get everyone's attention)* I see everyone's here. The best was saved for last. *(She laughs at her joke; no one else is quite sure it was funny)*

Snictnity: You are late.

Van Zahnt: I certainly hope you haven't started without me. *(Crosses to sit at the table)*

Minister: Oh, no, we were waiting for everyone to arrive. *(Snictnity snorts in disgust)* Why don't we go ahead and get this meeting started? As you know, the building committee has already approved the plans for the new church building. Now it's time for you, our church's Landscape and Grounds Committee, to approve the plans. I'd like to introduce Mr./Ms. Jones, who is a nationally-known architect and landscape designer, and at this point I will let Mr. /Ms. Jones take over the meeting. Mr./Ms. Jones takes over the meeting. *(Everyone claps* as *the minister takes a seat at the table)*

Jones: Thank you. *(Jones begins to unroll the blueprints for all to see)* The church plans have been approved and so now it is time for the preliminary discussion on the landscape design. As you know, I believe that it is vitally important that the building and the landscape design interact as one, to create a unity of composition.

Snictnity: *(Quietly)* Also convenient for keeping all business within your company.

Van Zahnt: Shh!

Jones: Here you can see the outline of the building. *(Points to various places on the blueprint)* The parking lot is located at the back with a play area located to the side. Because you chose an enormously large tract of land, a variety of landscape options are available to you.

Snictnity: We bought this large tract of land to allow for expansion possibilities in future years. Therefore, I don't see that we need a very detailed landscape plan. It seems to me, we should just bulldoze the entire tract. Put some grass all around with maybe just a few bushes up by the building. Then, when we need to add-on, the land is all ready to go.

Van Zahnt: I disagree entirely. Our church has a responsibility to present a beautiful face to the world, so that anyone driving by would be interested in attending. It is also important for current members to take pride in the appearance of the church. We wouldn't want to suffer any embarrassment from looking too plain or ordinary. I have been meeting with my garden club, and we have devised a list of plants, trees, and shrubs that should be used to beautify the church. *(Pulls several sheets of paper out of her purse, which she hands to Jones)* Now I am sure when you read through this list, you will recognize the experience and expertise that went into the selection of these plants, some of which are truly exotic and expensive, I might add. Naturally I would be willing to contribute some additional funds to the Building And Grounds budget, to ensure that the quality and size of vegetation selected is suitable for our church's needs. *(Hands a check to the minister)* You can see that I have earmarked the check for the appropriate use of the funds. Well, I think that takes care of just about everything. Shall we adjourn?

Snictnity: Although I am in favor of an efficient meeting, I am certainly not going along with your hare-brained notion of sticking weird plants everywhere, when we will just have to bulldoze them in a year or two.

Van Zahnt: *(Gasps)* You most certainly will not be bulldozing my lovely and expensive flowers.

Janet: *(Gently)* Just a minute. I thought this was supposed to be a committee meeting and a committee decision, with guidance from the designer. I don't believe I agree with either of you. I think that —

50

Snictnity: Listen, since this is your first committee as a member of this church, perhaps you should just listen and learn.

Van Zahnt: Well, I am surprised that we agree on something. Dear girl, I doubt that you have the experience or the funding to vastly influence the decision that is made here, so —

Snictnity: I know for a fact, that no donation is going to be the determining factor on the decision here, so you can just think —

Minister: Just a minute. Perhaps we should all take a deep breath and let the designer explain any ideas that he/she has.

Jones: Well, generally I like to meet with my clients first, to get an idea of their areas of interest and budget, before submitting a suggested plan. I think I have an understanding of Mr. Snictnity's and Mrs. Van Zahnt's position, but I don't believe I have heard from all.

Janet: Thank you! I would like to see, as much as possible, the original indigenous trees and plants left intact. This would allow for a greater appreciation of God's creation through the native plants and wildlife. Perhaps since we have so much land, a nature area with a walking trail through, so the children could learn more —

Snictnity: Oh, no, it's one of those kook environmentalists. They always slow up the process and won't allow any construction. This meeting should have been over some time ago. *(Looks at his watch)* I simply don't have any more time. I have to go. Please notify me of the next meeting. I will put the date on my Daytimer. *(Leaves)*

Van Zahnt: This is simply ridiculous, as if I am going to fund some sort of nature area. I don't know who selected these people for the Landscape Committee, but obviously a grievous error has been made. *(Takes the check back, and heads for the door)* I take it the error will be corrected before the next meeting.

Jones: *(Bewildered)* Wasn't this supposed to be a church committee meeting?

(Blackout)

Cooking With Carol

Scriptures: John 6:24-35
John 6:35, 41-51

Cast Of Characters
Announcer: either sex, very friendly, warms up the audience for Carol
Carol: an energetic television hostess who is a success

(The lights come up on the announcer in front of a table filled with cooking utensils and ingredients. Off to one side, signs reading "applause" and "laugh" can be seen)

Announcer: Hello, studio audience! In a few minutes we'll be going on the air. So, be sure that you clap and laugh when given the appropriate cues. Now, don't be nervous. I'm here to guide you through the show and I'll be chatting with you on commercial breaks. *(Looks offstage)* I'm getting the signal from the stage manager, five seconds to show, four, three, two ... *(Announcer hits the mark and gives a big smile)* Ladies and gentlemen, thank you for tuning into ... "Cooking with Carol." And now, the person you've been waiting for ... that culinary cultivator, the leader in kitchen culture ... It's Carol! *(Points to the applause sign, and leads the audience)*

Carol: *(Enters waving to several sections of the audience. Announcer continues to work hard to keep the applause going until she signals enough)* Oh, thank you! What a welcome! Thank you so much! Well, you don't want to stop applauding today, do you?

Hello, America! *(Signals an end for the applause)* Thanks for such a warm welcome. Obviously they know what a special show I have planned for them today, don't they?

Announcer: I'm sure they do, Carol. What are you cooking today?

Carol: Today we're making bread. But not just any bread —

Announcer: No, I'm sure you'd never make plain, boring white bread.

Carol: Not me! Today we're making sourdough bread.

Announcer: Wow! What a treat! *(Signals applause)*

Carol: Well, let's get to it. *(Steps behind the counter/table and holds up a bowl to show the camera)* Sourdough bread requires what we call a starter.

Announcer: A starter?

Carol: That's right. Mine was given to me years ago, by a very special friend.

Announcer: How long ago was that, Carol?

Carol: More years than I would care to admit. *(Announcer laughs and points to the laugh cue)* And for a lucky few of the audience today, I'm going to give them a bit of my own personal starter.

Announcer: Oh, Carol, what a gift! *(Points to the applause sign)* How nice of you to share your treasure!

Carol: Isn't it? *(Holds a recipe card up)* Let me hold this so the camera can get a close up of the recipe. You need one cup of sourdough starter, two-and-one-half cups all-purpose flour, not self-rising, everyone, and two cups of warm water about 105 to

115 degrees. Now mix those first ingredients in a glass bowl with a wooden spoon. Cover, then let stand in a warm, draft-free place eight hours.

Announcer: *(Super cheerfully)* Eight hours! We have to wait eight hours?

Carol: That's right! Even with all the right ingredients put together properly, it takes time to get it right. But of course, I have previously prepared some. So, let me just pull that out. *(Searches, but can't seem to find it)* Let me see —

Announcer: Well, Carol, while you're busy maybe we should take a commercial break?

Carol: *(Frantically)* What? *(Stops looking and faces out)* Oh, yeah, that would be perfect.

Announcer: Now, don't touch that dial. We'll be back in a just minute with more "Cooking with Carol."

Carol: *(With a huge change in personality)* Will someone please tell me where the — *(Yells offstage)* Fred, where is the stuff? Like I am standing up in front of millions of people without any dough. I'm going to kill Fred.

Announcer: *(Whispers)* Carol, let's not forget our studio audience.

Carol: Look, if I don't find that bread, it won't matter if there is a studio audience or not. *(Announcer gives her a look)* Oh, I'm sure they already know I don't actually cook; I just tell people how to do it. *(Goes offstage)* As if I haven't already had a bad day, now this!

Announcer: Well, ladies and gentlemen, I hope you've enjoyed your experience so far. I know it is probably a surprise that Carol didn't fix the dough herself, but she is such a busy person that she doesn't really have time to take care of all the details in life. Are there any questions from the audience I can answer?

Carol: *(Comes back in with a bowl with dough in it)* No questions, don't do that right now!

Announcer: Well, maybe you're right. Only one more minute, and we will be back live.

Carol: Well, I've got the stuff. So, at least we're ready to move on with the rest of the recipe. Have you ever had one of those days?

Announcer: *(Looks offstage, moving into camera position)* We're getting the signal, five, four —

Carol: I wish there was a recipe for getting through life. Then I could just follow the directions.

Announcer: Welcome back, everyone! Let's get some more fascinating details on bread.

(Blackout)

Searching

Scriptures: John 6:51-58
John 6:56-69

Cast Of Characters
Narrator: male or female, any age
Woman: female, high school age or older
Actor: any age older than college; looks slick
Actress: any age older than college; looks funky

(The lights come up on empty area with the Narrator sitting on a stool to one side. As the narrator opens his book and begins to read, the action is presented by the characters)

Narrator: Once upon a time there was a young woman searching. *(The young woman enters looking around)* She wasn't sure what she was searching for, but she wanted something more. She felt lost. *(She stops, puzzled)* One day she came across a man promising great things. *(A man enters carrying a box full of bottles)* He was selling a special elixir out of the back of his SUV. *(He pulls out a bottle and gestures wildly)* This special stuff called "Invigorate" promised all sorts of wonderful things. It cured depression. It gave you energy. It made life special. So, the young woman bought a bottle and tried it. *(She hands the actor some money and drinks from the bottle)* It tasted great! So, she bought a case. *(She hands the actor more money and he hands her the box. He walks offstage counting his money)* She drank another bottle. She drank a bottle every day for a week. *(The young woman moves to several areas on the stage, and drinks a bottle)* But the young woman couldn't tell any difference, except maybe her hair seemed a little more shiny.

So, she continued a search. *(An actress enters in far-out clothes, wearing a lot of crystals)* Next, she met a woman who seemed free of inhibitions. *(The actress sits down in a yoga position and meditates, oohing and ahhing)* The young woman watched the other woman for a while as she meditated. Then the young woman asked, "Why do you do that?" *(The actress stops her noises and looks at the young girl showing her a crystal)* "I am calling out to the crystal and harnessing the power of the crystal," the woman explained. "Here, you try it! It will make you live longer," she said. "You will love it." *(The young woman sits next to the actress, while the actress gives one of her crystals to the young woman. Both begin making silly oohs and ahhs)* But it didn't work for the young woman. She just felt silly! So, the young woman thanked her and watched as her meditating friend went on her way. *(The actress leaves)* So now, the young woman was still lost and getting very depressed. She still hadn't found what she wanted. *(The young woman stops in thought)* What exactly did she want?

She decided she needed to be healthier. That would take care of her problems. She probably wasn't eating right. She needed to go to the health food store and stock up. *(She crosses to where the actor is miming working at a health food store)* So, with the help of the clerk, she bought 47 different vitamins and fifteen different herbs to be taken three times a day. *(The two mime picking out bottles and then the young woman pays before she leaves the pretend store)* Surely that would make her feel healthy, satisfied, and whole. So, a lot poorer, she went home to try her new pills. *(The young woman looks through all her pills and takes some)* But it was confusing, and time consuming, and you had to drink a lot of water. *(She drinks some more)* She drank a lot of water to get all those pills down. *(She drinks some more)* Did I say a lot of water? *(She drinks some more)* So, after a while, when she couldn't tell any difference, she stopped taking the pills and threw them out.

By now, she was feeling lost, depressed, and poor. What is it that's missing in my life? she wondered. How can I be healthy and live happily ever after? she thought. What am I searching for?

(Blackout)

The Deeds

Scriptures: James 1:17-27
                        James 2:14-17

Cast Of Characters
Minister: male or female any age over college
Members: male or female played in a rotating manner. You can use
as few as two, or as many as ten, with each person circling around
behind to the end of the line.

---

*(The lights come up on the minister standing center stage, greeting
and shaking hands with all of the church members, as if after the
service. Actors should bring a prop, which signifies the deed/job
they are talking about and give the item to the minister. The minister has an increasingly difficult time trying to shake everyone's
hand)*

Minister: So glad you came today.

Member 1: Thank you. Say, I couldn't help but notice that the
trash can needed emptying. *(Hands the minister the trash can and
leaves)*

Minister: *(Continues to hold the trash can throughout)* How are
you today?

Member 2: I'm fine. I just thought I would mention that this Bible
has a torn page that needs to be taped up. *(Hands the Bible to the
minister and leaves)*

Member 3: A fine sermon today, except, of course, the parts I slept through. *(Laughs)*

Minister: *(Laughs)* Well, thank you.

Member 3: Just kidding. By the way, I noticed there was a visitor sitting in my row.

Minister: Oh, wonderful. Did you greet him?

Member 3: No, but I wanted to be sure you knew, so you could take care of him. *(Leaves)*

Minister: I'm so pleased you came today.

Member 4: Well, thank you. I guess it has been a while. Listen, I thought I should bring to your attention, that the pencil in the church pew in my aisle was used down to the nub. *(Hands the pencil to the minister)*

Member 5: Well, at least your row had a pencil. We didn't have anything to write with in our row.

Minister: Would one of you be able to go to the office and get some pencils out?

Member 4: Oh, no, I couldn't. I barely had enough time in my schedule to attend church. *(Leaves)*

Member 5: Well, maybe next time. Today I have to leave right away to meet someone for lunch. *(Leaves)*

Minister: We're glad to have you here.

Member 6: Why, thank you! Say, my neighbor has been sick for about a month. I was wondering if you could call on her, just to pick up her spirits a little.

Minister: Of course, I'd be happy to visit her.

Member 6: Oh, great! Her name is Mrs. Rodgers; she spells it with a *d*. And her house is just to the right of mine.

Minister: Have you been spending a lot of time with her, since her illness?

Member 6: Oh, no, I just don't have the talent for being around ill people. *(Leaves)*

Minister: How is your arthritis?

Member 7: It seems to be pretty good today. I wanted to let you know that the church newsletter arrived folded improperly and torn. *(Hands the newsletter to the minister)* Just look at it! *(The newsletter is folded wrong, with a small tear)*

Minister: I had to fold the newsletters this week because no one showed up to help.

Member 7: Well, that is a problem. Anyway, I would appreciate it if you called the post office and spoke to them about handling the church mail with more care. *(Leaves)*

Member 8: Speaking of the church's newsletter, I don't seem to be receiving a copy. Could you please check to be sure my address is correct on the mailing list?

Minister: Is your address correct in the church directory?

Member 8: Well, I don't know. I've never looked. However, you or the secretary could verify my correct address in the telephone book.

Minister: I just happen to have a copy of this week's newsletter here. *(Still holding everything)* Would you like to take this copy?

Member 8: No, thank you, it's used! Just stick a fresh one in the mail. *(Leaves)*

Minister: Sorry, I'm having a little difficulty shaking your hand.

Member 9: Oh, don't worry about that. I was just wondering how to hand you this hymnal. Unfortunately, someone has marked with a pencil on several of the pages, probably a child. You'll need to go through and erase them.

Minister: Do you know where the scribbles are located?

Member 9: No, you'll just have to look through the whole book. *(Places the hymnal on the edge of the trash can)* There you go, now walk carefully. *(Leaves)*

Member 10: Last, but definitely not least. Quite an armload you have there! Did you notice the offering plates were still sitting on the table?

Minister: Well, no, but the money will need to be counted.

Member 10: Just thought I'd mention it. Well, I'm out of here. Have a good week! *(As he leaves, he pats the minister on the arm, and dislodges everything, which falls to the floor)*

(Blackout)

The Applicants

Scripture: James 2:1-10

Cast Of Characters
Secretary: male or female over college age
Applicant 1: any age, shabbily dressed
Applicant 2: any age, very richly dressed

(The lights come up on a secretary who is seated at a desk in an office and hard at work. Applicant 1 enters and glances around hesitantly. The secretary looks the applicant over with distaste and then quickly turns away, looking busy. Finally Applicant 1 approaches the desk)

Applicant 1: Excuse me for interrupting your work, but I need some assistance. I was interested in becoming a member. Can you tell me what I need to do?

Secretary: *(Sighs)* Are you sure this is the right place for you?

Applicant 1: Well, I think so.

Secretary: If you will excuse me for saying so, you don't fit the usual profile.

Applicant 1: I didn't know there was a specific ... what did you call it?

Secretary: Profile, you know.

Applicant 1: No, I didn't know. I thought everyone was welcome. Does this mean I can't join?

Secretary: *(Irritatedly)* If you are going to be insistent about it, I guess you can fill out an application.

Applicant 1: An application?

Secretary: Yes, to see if you fit the qualifications. *(Pulls out an application and clipboard, which she hands to the applicant)* Why don't you take a seat in the corner over there? *(Gestures to a folding chair in the back corner)*

Applicant 1: *(Takes a seat and reads the first question)* "What is the name of your sponsor?" Excuse me, is a sponsor required?

Secretary: It's not *required*, just preferred.

Applicant 1: Well, that's good, because I don't have one. *(Pauses)* "What is your annual income?" Do I have to answer that?

Secretary: No, it says right there on the form that you may choose not to answer any of the questions. However, any blank spaces will impact the decision on whether you're allowed to become a member. Listen, I really need to get some work done. Why don't you just fill out what you can by yourself, and then get back to me?

Applicant 1: *(Politely)* Oh, okay. Sorry I bothered you. *(Both people work quietly for a minute, then Applicant 2 enters)*

Secretary: *(Looks Applicant 2 over, then immediately speaks)* Can I help you?

Applicant 2: Yes, I was interested in becoming a member.

Secretary: Oh, that's wonderful! Let me just get the application out. *(Pulls out the form)*

Applicant 2: John Watkins suggested I come here, and give the place a try.

Secretary: John did? *(Writes the name down in the sponsor's blank)* John is truly a wonderful guy, isn't he?

Applicant 2: Yeah, seems like he's got it all. A nice job, great car, and have you seen his home?

Secretary: Oh, yes, isn't it wonderful! We went out to his house for a meeting one time. *(Gets out of her chair and walks toward a couple of upholstered chairs)* You can have a seat here while you fill out the information, if you like. Now, I have already filled in your sponsor, since John recommended you.

Applicant 2: Thanks a lot.

Secretary: Now, don't feel like you have to answer any of the questions that make you feel uncomfortable. This really isn't an official application. It is just for informational purposes, so that we can serve you better in the future. If you have any questions, please feel free to ask me, and I'll help you all that I can.

Applicant 2: Say, that's really nice of you.

Secretary: *(Returns to the desk, still talking to Applicant 2)* Would you like a cup of coffee to drink?

Applicant 2: No, but thanks for asking.

Applicant 1: *(Crosses back to the secretary's desk, still polite)* Here's my application, and your pen.

Secretary: Thank you. *(Takes the clipboard and glances over the paper)* But you've hardly filled anything out? I just don't know if you'll be allowed to join with so few answers completed.

Applicant 1: That's okay. I think you're right. I'm not sure I'd fit in here. *(Leaves, walking past Applicant 2)*

Secretary: *(Happily)* Well, if you're sure.

Applicant 2: Oh, my gosh! Do you know who that was?

Secretary: Just some person wasting my time.

Applicant 2: Didn't you read the newspaper yesterday? I don't know for sure, but he/she looked just like that eccentric that gave away a million dollars to charity.

(Blackout)

The Grocery Store

Scriptures: James 3:1-12
Mark 9:30-37

(The lights come up on a woman, sitting on the couch talking on the telephone)

Oh, I agree. How typical. Wait till I tell you what happened to me the other day at the grocery store. You know, the one that's up the street, on the corner. Ohhh, what's the name? *(Pauses as if listening to a response)* Yeah, that's the one. Anyway, I was in such a hurry that day, so I ran in and picked up just a few items. I get in the express lane, you know, twelve items or less. And the person who is not directly in front of me, but the next person, has a cart full. I mean, there had to be at least twenty items, basically double the number. Talk about a counting problem. I really wish people would be a little more considerate of other people; nowadays all they think about is themselves. I mean I was buying some milk, bread, butter, and several bunches of bananas, but the bananas are all one thing, so that just counts as one item. Right? ... *(Pauses as she waits for an answer)*

The next thing I know, she is arguing with the clerk about a coupon. Something about not having the right size item. I mean, please, doesn't the store have a responsibility to tell that lady to get in a regular checkout line instead of the rest of us being forced to wait forever ... *(Pauses)* ... I know, I know, but wait, I haven't even gotten to the best part of the story. Guess who it was? Oh, you'll never guess ... no ... guess again ... it was Mrs. Crispin. You know, the lady at church who is so pious, she scrunches up her face ...

67

(Disgustedly) No, she did not get that way from drinking prune juice ... She got that way from always being so proper, and doing everything correctly. And there she is at the grocery store lying, sinning no less, about the number of items she has. And for what? So she can go through the express lane. I mean, let me tell you, when I sin I want to get a little more out of it than going through the express lane. Do you think she put that in her prayers at night? "Dear God, please forgive me for lying, so I could go through the express lane."

Nooo! I didn't know her son was still at home! *(Laughs)* Is he a typical mama's boy? Oh really, when did the car accident ... When he was twelve years old ... that's terrible ... So, how long has she paid someone to watch her son, while she runs errands? I know what you are trying to say, that maybe she had a good reason for being in a hurry. But whether you have a good excuse or not, a lie is still a lie, isn't it? I needed to get home and fix dinner. Harold just throws a fit if I don't have his supper ready for him when he gets home.

Did I ever tell you about Doris? No? Well, let me tell you —

(Blackout)

The Pray-er

Scripture: James 5:13-20

Cast Of Characters
Mildred: an elderly lady who is handicapped
Lucy: a young volunteer with an attitude

(As the lights come up, Mildred is seated in a chair, knitting. Her walker is close beside her. There is a knock at the door)

Mildred: It's open. Come on in.

Lucy: Mildred, you are supposed to wait until I call out the name of the company. You know the policy. Don't just tell anyone to come in. Hey, you didn't know it was me. It could have been a robber or a thief.

Mildred: Well, they probably would have just come right in without waiting for an invite.

Lucy: How many times have you been told to ask who it is first?

Mildred: More times that I can count. *(Exasperatedly)* I'll try to do better the next time you come over.

Lucy: *(Patronizingly)* Should I go back out and knock again so you can practice?

Mildred: No, dear, I think I can handle it.

Lucy: Well, all right, if you're sure?

Mildred: I'm sure. It's my feet that don't work, not my brain.

Lucy: Well, here is your lunch.

Mildred: Thank you, dear. *(Starts to eat)*

Lucy: *(Sits. There is a long pause while Lucy tries to think of something to say)* I guess I don't know anything new.

Mildred: You don't need to stay, Lucy. I'm sure you'd rather be doing other things.

Lucy: No, it's okay. I'm supposed to put some time in at each house. *(Notices a list written on a sheet of paper sticking out of the Bible)* Hey, this has my name written on it. Were you going to report me or something?

Mildred: No, I wasn't going to report you. Why don't you go ahead and pull the list out and see what it says by your name.

Lucy: It says, "Take away the hurt." *(Defensively)* What's that supposed to mean?

Mildred: It means that I wish whatever is upsetting you would go away.

Lucy: I never said I was upset.

Mildred: No, you didn't. Maybe it was just my imagination that something was bothering you.

Lucy: *(Reluctantly)* No, it wasn't your imagination.

Mildred: Do you want me to stop praying for you?

Lucy: Is that what this whole list is?

Mildred: Yes, people that I know or have heard about that need prayers.

Lucy: I didn't ask you to pray for me.

Mildred: No, you didn't. I wanted to pray for you.

Lucy: Why? We don't even get along all that well.

Mildred: It's something I can still do that's useful.

Lucy: It's weird. You hardly know me and you're praying for me. Why don't you do something else?

Mildred: Because I'm not like you. I can't go around house to house to take meals or serve someone in need. I just sit here all day, bored to tears.

Lucy: Yeah, well, I better get going.

Mildred: Heavens, yes, you wouldn't want to stay a minute over your required time.

Lucy: You know, I don't do this because I want to.

Mildred: Nobody's forcing you.

Lucy: Yeah, they are. I have to do so many hours of community service.

Mildred: Why?

Lucy: Mind your own business. *(Starts to leave, then stops)* My girlfriend got caught stealing.

71

Mildred: But you weren't doing anything wrong?

Lucy: No, I wasn't. I asked her to put the shirt back and she told me she did.

Mildred: But she didn't?

Lucy: No, she didn't. It's all her fault I have to do this stuff. She jerked me around.

Mildred: I'm sorry. I guess being lied to hurt.

Lucy: Whatever.

Mildred: See you tomorrow?

Lucy: Yeah. *(Leaves. After a moment she knocks)*

Mildred: Who is it?

Lucy: *(Comes back into the room)* You remembered!

Mildred: Like it did me any good. You just walked right on in.

Lucy: Yeah, you're right.

Mildred: So, what did you come back for?

Lucy: Never mind. *(Starts to leave, then hesitates)* Will you keep praying for me?

Mildred: Of course.

(Blackout)

The Hotel And Restaurant

Scriptures: Hebrews 1:1-4
Hebrews 4:12-16
Daniel 12:1-4 (alternative)

Cast Of Characters
Peter: the *maitre d' hotel*, middle-aged or older
Customer 1: any age or sex, older than Customer 2
Customer 2: a younger woman
Customer 3: a female senior citizen

(The lights come up on Peter in a tux, standing in front of an elegant doorway. Two chairs and an end table are off to one side. Next to Peter is an elaborate table or podium holding a book and a telephone, which starts ringing)

Peter: *(Answers the phone)* Heaven's Gate Hotel and Restaurant, where the food is divine, and the rooms are out of this world. This is Peter speaking. May I help you? ... *(Snaps to attention, because he is speaking to THE BOSS)* You need to add a name to the reservation list? Excellent sir, the name ... Roberta Denter ... *(Writes the name in the book)* Very good, sir, I have the name logged as requested ... Always a pleasure talking to you, sir. Have a glorious day! *(Customer 1 enters)* Welcome to Heaven's Gate Hotel and Restaurant, where the food is divine, and the rooms are out of this world. May I help you?

Customer 1: Yes, I'd like a room and a table for lunch, please.

73

Peter: Excellent! Your name, please.

Customer 1: *(Ignores Peter's question)* I've heard such wonderful things about this establishment. I can't wait to experience them for myself.

Peter: Do you have a reservation?

Customer 1: No, but that shouldn't be a problem. I doubt you're that busy.

Peter: Well, generally speaking, we do require reservations.

Customer 1: All right, fine. If that's the way you're going to be, I'll just make my reservation now. Party of one, and I'd like a seaside view if possible, non-smoking.

Peter: It isn't that simple. You see, first you need —

Customer 1: Sir, let's not be ridiculous. I can see through the doorway that there is plenty of room. *(Pulls out some cash)* Now, you just let me know how much for a window table.

Peter: You don't understand —

Customer 1: Just name the price.

Peter: I'm afraid that our reservations can't be purchased. I'm very sorry. *(Customer 1 walks off in a huff. The phone rings)* Heaven's Gate Hotel and Restaurant, where the food is divine, and the rooms are out of this world. May I help you? ... You'd like to make a reservation? *(Still talking on the phone, with a nod acknowledges Customer 2 entering. Customer 2 seems confused, and continually looks around)* Excellent, there is one in your party, I take it? Oh, just a guess. *(Customer 3 enters and is very impatient)* Can you tell me a little about yourself? Well, I'm sorry ... Yes, I have heard of the right to privacy ... I really think you should speak with my

74

BOSS ... Oh, it's no trouble. He always has time for anyone and everyone ... Just a moment and I'll transfer you. *(Hangs up the phone, while Customer 3 paces and fumes)*

Customer 3: Well, I must say, the service isn't at all what I expected from such an upscale place.

Peter: Sorry, to keep you both waiting. Welcome to Heaven's Gate Hotel and Restaurant. May I help you?

Customer 3: You certainly may. My name is Paula Whitfield, party of one.

Peter: Thank you, but I believe this other customer was here first. If you will just allow me to take care —

Customer 3: *(To Customer 2)* I really am in a hurry. Do you mind if he helps me first, dear?

Customer 2: No, not at all.

Customer 3: I'm meeting someone here, and I just can't wait.

Peter: *(Checks the book)* Whitfield, you said?

Customer 3: Yes, that's right.

Peter: I'm sorry, I can't find your reservation.

Customer 3: But that's not possible. I'm sure it must be there. Look again!

Peter: *(Looks)* No, it isn't there.

Customer 3: How can that be? Let me see that book. *(Peter shows Customer 3 the entry)* My name isn't there. There must be some mistake. *(Stunned, she walks over and collapses in the chair)* I did

75

all that charity work for nothing. I didn't even like participating, but I knew I needed to volunteer.

Peter: *(To Customer 2)* Your name, please?

Customer 2: Oh, I'm probably not in the book. Maybe I haven't done enough for other people either. I'm not sure what I'm doing here.

Peter: I'd be happy to check for your name.

Customer 2: Well, I guess it wouldn't hurt to look. My last name is Ashton, Jenny Ashton.

Peter: Just a moment, please. *(Flips through the book to the A's)*

Customer 2: If I do have a reservation, it's only because someone else called ahead for me. You know, paid my dues.

Peter: Yes, that does happen. Jennifer E. Ashton, you have a reservation. Congratulations, Jenny!

Customer 2: *(Excitedly)* Oh, my gosh!

Peter: If you'll follow me. *(Leads her toward the door)* So, who do you think called ahead for you?

(Blackout)

The Mission

Scriptures: Mark 10:17-31
Proverbs 3:13-18 (alternative)

Cast Of Characters
Agent 1: male or female, any age
Agent 2: male or female, any age
Subject: senior citizen, male or female

(The lights come up on an empty park bench. Agent 1, in a trench coat, is pretending to be out for a casual stroll. Agent 2 walks on stage and stands to one side. Then holding an earpiece, Agent 1 speaks into the microphone)

Agent 1: *(Whispers)* I'm here.

Agent 2: *(Speaks into Agent 1's earpiece, not seen only heard)* Listen, rookie, the appropriate response is, I am in position.

Agent 1: Sorry, I forgot. I guess I'm a little nervous.

Agent 2: We have a walking subject in the scope, ETA to your position, two minutes.

Agent 1: Huh? Someone's coming?

Agent 2: Brilliant, Sherlock Holmes. May I recommend that you brush up on your jargon, or did you skip that class at the academy?

Agent 1: No, it's just this is my first assignment. Say, how come I'm out in the open? Couldn't I have watched from the surveillance van?

Agent 2: The rookie is always out in the field. That way if the rookie survives, we know to spend more tax dollars for your training. Subject is an older male approximately 6 feet 180 pounds, and is wearing gray. *(Insert description that is appropriate to casting)* He/she matches the description of expected subject, but no one has actually ever seen the person. Warning! Subject is carrying a briefcase.

Agent 1: Oh, great, my first time out, and I get a subject with a briefcase. *(Pauses)* So, what's wrong with someone carrying a briefcase?

Agent 2: *(Disgustedly)* The case could contain a weapon or a bomb.

Agent 1: No hope for just some legal documents?

Agent 2: ETA of subject to our scanner is ... Now! *(Pauses)* Rookie, today is your lucky day; we registered no major weapons and no bombs.

Agent 1: Thank you, God!

Agent 2: Of course, he could have plastik. Plus, our scanner doesn't acknowledge any of the microscopic munitions.

Agent 1: *(Sarcastically)* Gee, thanks. Why bother?

Agent 2: Hey, rookie, is that sarcasm I hear? You'd better be nice to your life-line. In the agency, I'm all you've got, buddy.

Agent 1: I'll remember that.

Agent 2: Just be sure you remember the opening code phrase.

Agent 1: I know it. You made me practice it a million times. I'm ready.

Agent 2: Great, because subject is upon you. *(Subject enters the stage and sits on the bench)* Just remember, I'm only a block away, and I'll be listening with you all the way. I'm voicing off now, unless you have an emergency.

Agent 1: *(Crosses over and sits on the other end of the bench, then whispers)* I'm looking for Wisdom, for she is more profitable than silver and ... yields better returns than gold.

Agent 2: Rookie, why are you whispering? *(Subject can not ever hear Agent 2)*

Agent 1: *(There was no response from the subject, so Agent 1 speaks louder)* Hello?

Subject: I'm sorry. Were you speaking to me?

Agent 1: Yes, yes, I was.

Subject: I'm sorry; you'll have to speak up. I don't hear very well.

Agent 1: I said: I'm looking for Wisdom, for she is more profitable than silver and yields better returns than gold.

Subject: Say, I kind of like that greeting, much nicer than just talking about the weather.

Agent 1: *(Frustrated)* Do you know the response?

Subject: Response?

Agent 1: You know, the rest of it?

Subject: Sure, she is more precious than rubies, and nothing you desire can compare with her.

Agent 1: *(Hand on the earpiece, to Agent 2)* Well, is it a match?

Agent 2: Give me a second, I'm logging the response into the system. *(Typing on a keyboard can be heard)* Accepted, move to stage two.

Subject: I've been searching for wisdom all of my life. I pray to God that he would give me discernment, but I still haven't reached my full potential yet.

Agent 1: Huh? Oh, yeah, that's great, whatever. So, have you got the drop?

Subject: The drop? *(Laughs)* The way young people speak nowadays, I don't always recognize what you mean. But, yes, I think I've gotten the drop on things, just about got it all figured out. I have one more deed to do in my life. Then, I'm going to a senior care facility for what's left of my life.

Agent 1: This is your last job, huh? This is my first.

Subject: Congratulations. It's important to have a good job. Have you been looking for work long?

Agent 1: Well, it seems like I've been in the academy forever.

Subject: Money is always tight when you are studying, and when you first set out to make your mark in the world.

Agent 1: You got that right.

Agent 2: Enough with the chatting. Let's get the job done and get on back to the roost.

Agent 1: Huh?

Agent 2: Get the drop and let's go!

Agent 1: Oh, yeah, sorry. Well, if you wouldn't mind —

Subject: You know, I think you may be just the person to give this to. I wasn't sure of the best way ... *(Hands the briefcase over to Agent 1, and leaves)* Here, this is for you. Have a good life now, bye.

Agent 1: Thanks.

Agent 2: *(Urgently)* Rookie, did I see correctly? Did subject hand you the briefcase?

Agent 1: Sure, the scope is working fine.

Agent 2: Warning: we have a problem, proceed with extreme caution. The subject's drop is not proper. I repeat, not proper.

Agent 1: *(Anxiously)* He knew the code.

Agent 2: The listed drop was supposed to be an envelope.

Agent 1: *(Worriedly)* An envelope? Maybe it's in the briefcase?

Agent 2: Possibly, possibly not. Set the briefcase down very carefully. *(Agent 1 gently places the case on the bench)* Okay, now examine it with extreme caution. Do any of the locks appear to be tampered with?

Agent 1: No. Listen, if this is not what we are supposed to get, maybe we should just leave it here?

Agent 2: Oh, sure, let some innocent bystander happen onto the briefcase. Rookie, I'm surprised at you. What happened to "protect and defend"?

Agent 1: Okay, okay.

Agent 2: Go ahead and open the briefcase.

Agent 1: Shouldn't I stand guard until a bomb squad gets here?

Agent 2: The scanner showed no evidence of a bomb, and we don't have time —

Agent 1: *(In a panic)* I'm in no hurry.

Agent 2: Open it, rookie.

Agent 1: *(Carefully opens the briefcase, which is full of money and a note)* There's a whole bunch of money, and a note.

Agent 2: Well, since it didn't blow, why don't you read it?

Agent 1: *(Reads)* "To Whom It May Concern: I have sold all my possessions, because I no longer have need of them. The results are in this case. I trust you will spend the money wisely to help others. Remember, none of your actions are hidden from God's sight. May God bless your life, as he has blessed mine! Good luck on your mission."

(Blackout)

Are You Calling Me?

Scriptures: Hebrews 5:1-10
                    Mark 10:35-40

(The lights come up on a solitary figure, with no set or props. Blocking should be kept to a minimum, to encourage the interaction between the monologue and God)

Dear God: I remember when I was growing up, I used to talk to you a lot. I went to Sunday school, because it was fun. I said a little rehearsed prayer every night. *(Singsong)* "Now I lay me down to sleep, pray the Lord my soul to keep...." I bet you've heard it a million times. Then I got a little older, and I got more daring. I actually started asking you some questions. I never got answers. At least not from some booming voice that I recognized as God, you know, like from one of those Hollywood classics. I mean, I used to beg to hear your voice or an answer. I wanted the burning bush to appear right there, in my bedroom. But, it never did. So, I got tired of talking to the air. It seemed a little silly to me as I entered the teenage years.

So, I drifted away from you, and I grew up. When I started volunteering to fix up some old houses, I didn't really associate it with one of those life-changing moments. I mean, everybody at work was doing it. It was just one Saturday a year. We just did it because it was supposed to look good. Our boss was really promoting the project. Then later, I helped serve some food on Thanksgiving Day at a shelter. I really only did it because I'm single and don't have any family left. I didn't want to be alone the first Thanksgiving since my parents died. Eventually, I found myself volunteering someplace every week. Then, I started going to church, and even praying, talking to you again. I still didn't hear anything in the bedroom at night, when I prayed. But I still kept talking to you anyway, just in case you were listening.

Then yesterday at the office, I heard this voice. I looked around, but nobody was there. It was Saturday, and the office was closed. I was there by myself catching up on work. There wasn't any burning bush, but that's okay. I might have had a heart attack if I'd seen one. I could hear the voice just fine, and I heard exactly what was said. It made me realize that extra responsibilities come with the honor of hearing your voice. It scares me, and I need to know. Are you calling me?

(Blackout)

Three Words

Scripture: Mark 12:28-34

(The monologue can be done simply as a stand-alone, or use your imagination to create a set where someone chooses to have a conversation with God)

Dear God: Please forgive me. I've done something incredibly stupid. Or maybe it would be more accurate to say, I neglected to do something I should have done. It wasn't intentional, it just sort of didn't occur to me, exactly. Not until I read my Bible verse for the day. Then, it hit me over the head like a sledgehammer. I've read that same verse many times before. Other people have read that verse to me. Yet, I never realized. I'm probably not making this any better with my rambling.

Three basic words, on which nations have been lost and won. Feuds and families have been torn or mended by these words. Just three simple words, and yet I can't remember the last time I said them to you. I'm sure I must have spoken them. I can remember singing them to you. The lyricist at least got the message, even if I didn't. It's not as if I didn't mean the words; I did. If someone had asked me the question, I would have answered positively, faithfully, unswervingly, yes.

I just didn't think about saying them to you *every* day in the quiet of my prayers. I should have said it a million times through the years. *(Wryly)* After all, I don't hesitate to thank you for all the wonderful things that you've done for me. I frequently ask forgiveness for the many sins I've committed. I never fail to ask you for many favors for myself, my friends, and my church. I always ask for your guidance and protection. And yet I have failed you, yet again, when I could have given you a gift, so simple, and yet so wonderful.

Let me correct this error, once and for all, loud and clear with three glorious words. *I love you.* I know actions speak louder than words, and I pray I have done many things in the past to let you know how I feel about you. I pray that throughout the world in every language, there are a zillion voices yelling, "I love you." Not just singing your praises or thanking you for your gifts but saying, "I love you." How many times have I wanted to hear the words that I am loved? I expected these words of reassurance from you and other people. So, let me give them to you, Lord. I love you, with all my heart, my mind, and my soul. Amen.

(Blackout)

The Collection

Scripture: Mark 12:38-44

Cast Of Characters
Narrator: male or female, any age
Husband: male non-speaking role
Wife: female non-speaking role
Poor Woman: female non-speaking role
Usher: male or female non-speaking role

(The lights come up on an empty pew center stage, with stool to one side. All of the motions spoken by the Narrator should be acted out and exaggerated by the characters. The Narrator comes out and seats himself on the stool, then opens a book to read the following)

Narrator: Once upon a time there was a church. It was similar to many of God's churches. Every Sunday the church held services, which various people attended. People, creatures of habit, gravitated toward their usual pews or areas in the sanctuary. As usual, the Couple was one of the first to arrive. *(Husband can be seen walking on stage)* Well, just the Husband, really. He is a detail man, very precise, and a clock-watcher. *(Husband checks his watch)* Yes, he's right on time. The Husband carefully selects the same pew, where he always sits. *(Husband walks towards the pew and assesses the space)* After carefully allowing just enough room for his wife on the end, he sits down. He wouldn't want to allow too much room because then someone else might sit in his pew. His wife is usually a little late. *(Wife appears)* Especially if she sees someone to gossip with — *(Wife stops, hands on her hips, and* *glares towards Narrator)* Excuse me, "fellowship with" on the way into church. *(Wife rushes in to take her seat next to her husband)* The Wife walks quickly to her pew and takes her seat. Just in time, because the worship service has started. *(Husband checks his watch)* Yes, the minister has started on time. Both listen attentively, or at least appear to listen. Wife leans over and starts to tell her Husband the juicy tidbit she just learned. *(She leans over to whisper into his ear)* But Husband is already trying to concentrate on what he needs to accomplish at the office tomorrow. *(He brings his finger up to his chin and taps lightly, lost in thought)* Wife is irritated, because as usual he is not listening to her. *(She pokes him with her elbow)* Husband checks, yes, he has allowed sufficient space for her to sit without bumping into him. *(Husband checks the spacing, then glares at his wife)* He is about to reprimand her, when suddenly a woman appears at the end of the row. *(His mouth is open to speak to his Wife, when he sees the Woman standing hesitantly at the end of the aisle. Both Husband and Wife stare at the Woman)* Why is she standing at their pew? Can't she find somewhere else to sit? *(Couple glances around)* Unfortunately, the church seems to be rather full. Husband and Wife are going to have to share their pew today. They grudgingly slide toward the other end of the pew. *(Couple moves down)* The Woman smiles timidly and gratefully. Husband checks his watch. Yes, the Woman arrived very late. *(Husband and Wife look at his watch)* Wife nods in righteous agreement. After all, she arrived before the service started, barely. *(Wife glares again at the Narrator, who speaks to the audience)* Okay, just ignore the "barely." Both Husband and Wife begin to look over the pew invader. *(Both turn and look the Woman over head to toe)* The Woman appears to be dressed rather poorly. *(Husband and Wife look at each other in agreement, then scoot away from the Woman even more)* So, the Couple decides to move away from the Woman, who obviously is not dressed properly for church. The Woman nervously straightens her clothes, and grasps her handbag tightly against her. Her movement draws attention to her 99 cent purse, which she picked up at the Salvation Army Thrift Store. Husband and Wife scoot a little farther down the pew. Suddenly, the Usher appears on the end of the aisle. The Usher passes the plate to the Husband and Wife.

(Wife holds the plate, while Husband opens his wallet, and carefully selects his donation) The Husband, being the detail man that he is, wets his thumb and finger, and pulls out a crisp five-dollar bill. *(Husband should hold the money so the audience can clearly see)* He checks to be sure he only got one. Then, he wets his fingers again to pull out another five-dollar bill. Three times he carefully invades his billfold. He takes his time, so that everyone surrounding him may realize what a truly generous man he is. His Wife, sitting next to him, beams with pleasure at the generosity of her husband. She opens her purse and pulls out a rumpled twenty. She is employed too, and is not one to be outdone by her husband. The Wife then passes the plate to the Woman, being careful not to allow their fingers to touch. The Woman nervously takes the plate, which knocks her coin purse off her lap. Mortified the Woman watches as two pennies fall out onto the floor. Those two pennies are all the money that she has right now. Quickly she scoops the pennies up, and puts her money in the collection plate. She whispers reassuringly to herself, "The Lord will provide." *(Woman should mouth the words as the Narrator speaks)*

(Blackout)